Head on a Gleaming Plate

Also by Marina Tsvetaeva in Christopher Whyte's translations

Moscow in the Plague Year (Archipelago)
Milestones (Shearsman Books)
After Russia (The First Notebook) (Shearsman Books)
After Russia (The Second Notebook) (Shearsman Books)
Youthful Verses (Shearsman Books)

Marina Tsvetaeva

Head on a Gleaming Plate

August 1917–October 1918

translated from the Russian by
Christopher Whyte

Shearsman Books

First published in the United Kingdom in 2022 by
Shearsman Books Ltd
PO Box 4239
Swindon
SN3 9FN

Shearsman Books Ltd Registered Office
30–31 St. James Place, Mangotsfield, Bristol BS16 9JB
(this address not for correspondence)

www.shearsman.com

ISBN 978-1-84861-843-5

Introduction and translations
copyright © Christopher Whyte, 2022

The right of Christopher Whyte to be identified as the translator of this work has been asserted by him in accordance with the Copyrights, Designs and Patents Act of 1988.
All rights reserved.

Contents

Introduction	9
'From your arrogant Poland'	27
'A woodcutter has felled'	28
'Somebody left with a head on'	29
'Sleek-tongued fashion victims, we have not'	30
'No way! Hunger for love has not'	31
Joseph	32
'We looked each other in the eyes – no more'	34
'Blatant hunger's how I foot'	35
'Without God, without bread, without a home'	36
'Bothered by a light so late?'	37
'I've not forgotten the first day, infantile ruthlessness'	38
Peter's Horse Lets Fall a Hoof (*fragment*)	39
'One is a fop who's knocking at death's door'	40
'At evening families emerge'	41
'So, hundredweights of cares having been loaded'	43
'Eyemek Gwaroozim – the valley of roses'	44
'Oh, the fragrance'	45
'White, like the flour which they grind'	46
Rouen	47
'Gardens fill with blooms, then fade. The wind'	48
'There we stood, the two of us'	49

from **THE GREATCOAT**

(5) 'Chevalier de Grieux, don't waste'	50
(6) '*Beau ténébreux!* You're ill. Depressed. The world's'	50
(7) 'Machinations of nocturnal swallows'	51
(8) '"I bid farewell to Albion's foggy shores…"'	52
'I saw the new year in alone'	53

BROTHERS
'They lie asleep, still hugging close'	54
'Two angels, brothers robed in white'	54
'I gulp my salty tears back down'	55

'Wind resounding, wretched wind'	56
'You're leaving for a distant land'	57
'You stand alone before so many beauties'	58
'It must be five or six o'clock. A blue-grey haze. [Day breaks'	59
'Epoch of crowned intrigues, epoch'	60

from POEMS TO MY DAUGHTER
(4) '"Thank you, Marina, for the world!"'	61
(5) (i) 'I don't know where you end and I begin'	61
(ii) 'From church to church we go, not caring whether'	62
(iii) 'And as beneath the earth the grass'	62
(7) 'As if you were a baby bell'	62

'Groaning passion, groaning death'	64
'Sleep with his sickle passes by'	65
'A seraph and an eagle! There's some fight!'	66
'The pussy willow's glimmering down'	67
'A star can vindicate a snake'	68
'"Forgive me, my mountains!"'	69
'A rich man fell for a poor girl'	70
'The Lord endowed me with'	71
'You'd like to know what makes me rich?'	72
'I rinse the linen in the brook'	73
'Young men are ablaze'	74
'A cautious knock, three times repeated'	75
'I am. You'll be. Between us lies a chasm'	76
'Breadcrusts, suffering – the price is high!'	77
'When I lie dying, I won't say "I was"'	78
'Nights without the man I love – and nights'	79

'I spoke, a second person heard and whispered'	80
Remembering Béranger	81
'Air redolent of incense. Passing rain'	82
'I am the page your pen writes on'	83
'Remembering you is like thin smoke'	84
'My day is wanton and absurd'	85
'Midday lies leaden on the village'	86
'The heavy forehead droops, droops further, like'	87
'Some ears of corn are loaded, others scraggy'	88
'Young folk need spare no thought'	89
'Night's a nun, a female felon'	90
'Day is a broadly rustling cloak'	91
'You don't like me, nor do you'	92
'Verses proliferate, like stars and roses'	93
'My refuge from the savage hordes'	94
'Next they gave me mead to drink'	95
To Her Daïmon	96
'You are alien yet familiar'	97
'The forehead lifted towards the sky'	98
'Where honey lies, a sting lurks, too'	99
'Who failed to build a house'	100
'Writing and breathing'	101
'No need to talk to me. Here are'	102
'An officer strolls by with his sabre'	103
Eyes	104
'You arrive – at the table's edge'	105
'Place two flowers here upon	106
'These gifts were given me from the heavenly heights'	107
'Remove the pearl, my tears are left'	108
'Love! Love! Where have you ended up?'	109
'Autumn. An avenue of trees, like soldiers'	110
'You're the full moon, Persian girl, the crescent [moon's a Turk'	111
'Morning. Time for washing cups'	112
'Dearer to me than anything'	113

'Daughters make their hoops spin round'	114
'I'm not a troublemaker, I won't pour'	115
'It befits heroes to be frozen'	116

Notes   118

Introduction

The second revolution to shake Russia in 1917, which led to the Bolshevik takeover, happened between October 25th and November 2nd, according to the Julian calendar still in use then, which was thirteen days behind the Gregorian calendar applying further west in Europe. Tsvetaeva's husband Sergey Efron was serving in the 56th regiment, whose troops supported the revolt, while the officers remained faithful to their oath and did their best to defend the Kremlin against the insurgents. Tsvetaeva was travelling from the Crimea back to Moscow, a journey she would subsequently describe in a prose piece entitled 'October in a Railway Carriage', or perhaps 'The October Revolution in a Railway Carriage':

> Nothing to eat or drink for two and a half days and nights. (I feel that I am choking). Soldiers bring the newspapers – on pink paper. The Kremlin and all monuments have been blown up. By the 56th regiment. The buildings with the "junkers" and the officials who refused to surrender have been blown up. 16,000 dead. At the next station already 25,000. I say nothing. Smoke. One by one the other people travelling take a train in the opposite direction.

And shortly after:

> If God performs this miracle – leaves you among the living, I will follow behind you like a puppy.

The horrendous rumours proved to be unfounded. Tsvetaeva's movements in those tumultuous days are not easy to unravel. Having reached Moscow at dawn, she took a cab for which she had insufficient funds to Boris and Gleb Lane, where the house she had lived in with her husband and two daughters was situated. Challenged at the front door by two men in uniform, she learned that Sergey and the children, together with his sisters, were waiting for her at the home of friends:

> Not even once do I think about the children. If S. is not alive, then neither am I, and neither are they. Without me Alya cannot live, won't want to, won't be able. Like me without S.

That same evening, with Sergey and a friend of his, she caught a train southwards and, after seven days, reached Koktebel' on the Black Sea, in Crimea. It was November 10th and a snowstorm was in progress:

> A vision of Max V. with Ten on his knees, frying onions on the steps of the tower. And while the onions are cooking, a lecture, to Seryozha and myself, about Russia's fate tomorrow and the day after tomorrow.
> 'Now, Seryozha, this will happen and this… Bear it in mind.'
> And in insinuating tones, almost as if it makes him pleased, like a good enchanter talking to children, one image follows another – the entire Russian revolution for the next five years: terror, civil war, shootings, checkpoints, Vendée, savagery, distorted features, the spirit of instinctive energies freed from captivity, blood, blood, blood…

Max Voloshin was a burly, good-natured, shaggy-haired and bearded giant whose home close to the shore, together with the people who congregated in it, had played a vital role in Tsvetaeva's life in the years immediately preceding. It was there that she first encountered Sergey and, in her own highly romanticised account, asked him to select a pebble for her on the beach. His choice confirmed her decision that this man would become her husband. The day was May 5th, 1911. She was 18 and Sergey was 17. Three years later she wrote in a letter to Vasily Rozanov (March 7th 1914):

Our marriage bears so little resemblance to an ordinary marriage, that I don't feel married at all and haven't changed one bit – I love the same things and live in the same way as at seventeen. We shall never separate. Our meeting was a miracle.

If for neither of them the commitment to one another precluded other infatuations and involvements, this may reflect, beside their individual characters, the outlook of the milieu in which they met. Infidelity within marriage does not seem to have been viewed as a matter of major concern. Unless, as happened with Tsvetaeva in 1916, the other person involved was another poet known to be lesbian.

After a week Tsvetaeva wrote to her sister-in-law from Feodosiya, where she had taken lodgings for the winter, asking her to come south with the children. Otherwise she would come north herself. She did so on November 22nd 1917, upon which returning south became impossible.

*

Years of almost inconceivable deprivation and hardship followed. Orlando Figes at one point speaks of Tsvetaeva typing out the manuscripts of her friend and mentor Prince Volkonsky. What makes him imagine any item as luxurious as a typewriter would not long since have been pawned for food or fuel? Whatever Tsvetaeva copied out was done laboriously, by hand. A gifted poet from a privileged background was left to fend for herself and two small children in circumstances she was equipped neither by upbringing nor character to deal with. The downward gradient Tsvetaeva was engaged on would eventually lead to conditions she gives an account of in these notes from the "plague year", 1919, in an attempt to describe her daily routine:

> from there back to the kindergarten, to pick up lunch – from there – up the servants' stair, loaded down with little jugs, food boxes and jars – not a finger free!

followed by panic – what if the bag with the rationing cards has fallen out of the little basket? – up the servants' stair – and home. Right away, the stove. The embers are still smouldering. I blow on them. Heat all our food in a single saucepan – a soup resembling *kasha*. We eat. (If Alya is with me, the first thing I do is untie Irina from the chair. I started tying her up after she once, while we were away, took from the dresser half of a raw cabbage head and ate it.) I feed Irina and put her down to sleep. She sleeps in the blue armchair. I have a bed, but it won't come through the door. – I boil coffee. Drink it. Smoke. Write. Alya writes me a letter or reads. Silence for about 2 hours. Then Irina wakes up. We heat the leftovers. With Alya's help I recover what remains of the potatoes, sticking to the bottom of the samovar. Either me or Alya puts Irina to sleep. Then Alya goes to sleep.

At 10 the day is over. Sometimes I saw and chop wood for the next day. At 11 or 12 I too am in bed. Happy because of the little light just next to my pillow, the silence, my notebook, a cigarette, sometimes – bread.

With always, always, the forlorn hope of a knock at the downstairs door and a friendly visit. A thief who gained entry is supposed to have offered Tsvetaeva money because he was so appalled at the indigence he witnessed. Gradually she had retreated to the attic of a house they occupied entirely in the past:

> I have said nothing about the night-time journeys to the ground floor, terrifying because so cold – to what used to be Alya's nursery – to get a book I suddenly, madly desire, I have said nothing about what me and Alya are constantly, guardedly longing for: Did somebody knock at the door? I'm sure they are knocking! (The bell hasn't worked since the start of the Revolution, instead of a bell – a knocker. We live up at the top, beyond seven doors, and we hear everything: each scrape of someone else's saw, each blow of someone else's axe, each slamming

of someone else's door, each noise in the courtyard – everything, except a knock at our door!) And – all at once – they seem to be knocking! – either Alya, tossing on the little blue embroidered fur coat from when she was two, or me, with nothing on – downstairs, groping, rushing, in total darkness, first down the stair with no banister (they burned it) then down this staircase – towards the chain on the main door. (Actually, you can come in without any help from us, but not everybody knows.)

The poems featured here allow us to trace the beginnings of that process. Not merely an individual matter, it transformed the understandings and behaviours which had previously structured the society around her. 'No way! Hunger for love has not' and 'Sleek-tongued fashion victims, we have not' speak of a progressive breakdown in conventional sexual morality which Tsvetaeva's self-portrayals suggest she too took part in ('Blatant hunger's how I foot/ the bill for my last grand outlay!') Her view of love and passion had always been unrelentingly harsh, involving not so much a struggle for the survival of the fittest as a constant teetering on the brink of self-immolation ('I've not forgotten the first day, infantile ruthlessness') together with the unstoppable, sickeningly repetitive abuse of innocence: 'Upon those childish lips... a whole array of cannibals/ will hone the edge of beastly fangs'. What Joseph Brodsky spoke of as her Calvinist conscience meant that no one else's judgement on her antics could be harsher than her own ('White, like the flour which they grind').

It would, however, be a regrettable mistake to read these poems merely as expressions of the conditions under which Tsvetaeva found herself living. They can equally be viewed as a declaration of imaginative freedom in no way dictated by what was going on around her. Escapism, forlorn yet playful imaginings of other worlds, inaccessible in terms of either time or space, offered one way of coping with appalling deprivation. As was the case with many writers and intellectuals at the time, Tsvetaeva's speculations returned to the French Revolution, a similarly tumultuous upheaval in the course of history from which, hopefully, lessons could be gleaned – not least, regarding how long the convulsions were likely to last. The world before the Revolution fires Tsvetaeva's imagination, individuals and ways of life destined to disappear almost without trace ('Chevalier de Grieux, don't waste', 'Machinations of nocturnal swallows', 'Epoch of crowned intrigues, epoch'). She herself claimed that:

> From the first day of the revolution (February 28th) I already knew it: everything had gone. Understanding this, I offered no resistance.

That, she observed, made things easier. Besides the *ancien régime*, her alternative realities include a Spain where Jews and Christians can both be heretics ('Eyemek Gwaroozim – valley of roses'), Lord Byron on the vessel transporting him to Greece and a premature death ('"I bid farewell to Albion's foggy shores"'), or Joseph repulsing the advances of the wife of Potiphar, to whose predicament and suffering Tsvetaeva gives ample coverage ('Joseph').

Yet as the months proceed, and the first anniversary of the October Revolution looms near, the focus narrows, with Tsvetaeva producing a series of quintessential, stark yet tender lyrics focusing on moments from her everyday life which nonetheless acquire the timeless, distanced quality of archetypes ('Nights without the man I love – and nights', 'Verses proliferate, like stars and roses', 'Writing and breathing', 'Morning. Time for washing cups').

A further alternative world is early 15th century France, against which the drama of Joan of Arc's military exploits and death at the stake was played out. It is not difficult to see why Tsvetaeva found her such a seductive figure with which to identify. On the one hand the virgin in armour has an air of stubborn androgyny, plus a calling to self-immolation which allows no swerving from the path marked out. It is not hard to see in the 'winged associate' who whispers 'Sister, endure!' as the light of the flames starts being reflected in the martyr's shining armour another version of the pitiless, demanding male Muse and "daïmon" appearing elsewhere in Tsvetaeva's work ('Rouen'): 'I'm nothing now but Voice and Rage./ I became the Maid of Orleans'. Joan's virginity constitutes one pole of a vertiginous zig-zag between renunciation and profligacy as Tsvetaeva combines fastidiousness, needle-sharp perception, self-neglect and even head over heels self-abandonment. The identification becomes explicit in 'Midday lies leaden on the village'.

One element which marks these lyrics as belonging to an earlier phase in Tsvetaeva's poetic path is the lingering attraction of transgression. In the years of emigration after 1922, marginalisation and grinding poverty progressively sapped breaking the rules, flaunting one's deviation from the norm, wilfully defying convention of their meaning. The parade of exotic yet ultimately doomed lovers embraces 'a Jewish girl and a Spanish grandee', panama hats, cigars, London, Vienna and Monaco ('Oh, the fragrance'), a whole range of badly-assorted couples ('A rich man fell for a poor girl'), and a faithful wife accompanying her condemned husband to Siberia ('Without God, without bread, without a roof').

Tsvetaeva's debt to the German literature of Romanticism and after is all-pervasive and of crucial importance to the tonality achieved in her most piercing lyrics. Heine, an outsider thanks to his persistent irony and his Jewishness, was, she claimed, particularly akin. 'With evening families emerge' evokes the distinctly "kitsch" scene of a village in Germany as twilight falls, at the same time detailing the progressive, ineluctable corruption of a girl at the hands of a not further specified 'gentleman': 'The gentleman gives her his word... The gentleman kisses her lips'. The sacrifice of innocence on the altar of studied, cynical indifference is ubiquitous. Tsvetaeva's instinctive kinship with those who make light of poverty and marginalisation also accounts for the French poet Béranger figuring among her 'patrons' ('Remembering Béranger').

Her approach to gender is agnostic and defamiliarised. Joan's virginity is one element in the difficulty of assigning her to one gender or the other, not least because the refusal to concede herself to a man preserves her from the facile, apparently "natural" binaries of heterosexual pairing. A lyric like 'I am the page your pen writes on' can be read as abject, masochistic submission to male authority till one reflects that Tsvetaeva is playing with, and redefining, the relationship between a muse traditionally viewed as feminine and the poet who is a man (also present in the angel who whispers into Joan's ear as her martyrdom gets under way). The lyrics directly addressing a male lover are authoritative, even dictatorial. Nothing could be further from acknowledging an external, authoritative viewpoint in her opposite number ('I am. You'll be. Between us lies a chasm' or, in 'The Greatcoat' (6), 'Entrust the night that lies ahead to me... You've no inkling who I am').

Two persistent notes in the overall symphony, even if rarely highlighted or given centre stage, are the option of self-annihilation ('Remove the purple –/ I have my blood') and the unswerving commitment to composing verses ('Night, and a cast iron grille/ descends. Voices at war with wings'.) In one interpretation, the descending 'grille' could be the peremptory demands of metre and rhyme, the standards of an art which tolerates no shortcuts and abhors any hint of mediocrity.

Because her investigation of gender is both alienated and aleatoric, as something impossible to pin down definitively, a notional fixity whose inherent strangeness can never be tamed or rendered anodyne, Tsvetaeva is drawn to borderline instances of female abnegation and self-sacrifice. A feminity thus constituted is inherently unstable because so complicit in its own elimination from the world. These attitudes colour her approach to her own motherhood. At times she protests, viewing herself as a helpless victim, ruefully aware of her innate inadequacy to the role:

> Envying the empresses of fashion
> and little mites of dancers wearing tights,
> I contemplate years passing at the cradle,
> and fail to see the milk is boiling over!

A notebook entry reads: '"Don't call her Irina, call her Svetlana, Tamara..." Better to call her simply – Demon!' And shortly afterwards: 'Easier to be shut in a cage with a lion, than in a room with a breastfeeding child. (Irina, forgive me!)' The intensity of

Tsvetaeva's bond with her firstborn, Alya, can be alarming in its blurring of boundaries, even if it issued in the exquisitely delicate and chiselled lyrics from the cycle 'To My Daughter' included here. A chilling confession regarding Irina comes late in August 1918 (Old Style):

> Irina is one year and four months old. Half a year of her life (October and November, when I was in Crimea, and three months this summer) has been spent without me. I had faith in Alya from the very first minute, even before she was born, I dreamt (insanely!) about Alya. Irina was a *Zufallskind*. I feel no connection whatsoever to her. Where is this going to lead?

Zufallskind implies a child unplanned, effect of an accident. Ten days later an acquaintance would observe in a letter that

> In order to preserve any kind of passable relationship with Marina one must simply force oneself to forget that she has children, together with the ongoing implications of this unnatural state of things.

Where it led was to perhaps the most horrendous episode of the "plague year". Mistakenly convinced that they would be adequately cared for there, receiving the nutrition she was unable to assure them, Tsvetaeva entrusted both her daughters to a state orphanage at Kuntsevo outside Moscow. Alya, forbidden in the letters she wrote to refer to the poet as her mother, contracted malaria. Tsvetaeva took her home and nursed her through bout after bout of fever. Meanwhile in the orphanage Irina died of malnutrition. One wonders if, abandoned even by her sister in alien surroundings, the child simply ceased to eat. The date was February 2nd 1920. Tsvetaeva never returned to the place.

Elsewhere in the notebooks, Tsvetaeva playfully lists the advantages of living under the Bolsheviks. For example, if you wanted to die, all you needed to do, she claimed, was walk out into the street and shout: *Vive le roi!* She would later entrust a frantic examination of her conscience to these same notebooks, attributing the blame for what happened in part to her own addiction to adventure, in part to the harshness with which she treated herself, mistakenly imagining others would be able to match her own resilience. As much is hinted at in this elliptic observation: '"Love thy neighbour as thyself". And much good may it do him! Where I, and those like me, are concerned.' After a journey to the Bryansky Station (the entry is from August 27th and 28th 1918 (Old Style)) at half past 5 in the morning to get milk, she asked:

> What keeps me tormenting myself with these queues, cooperatives, the Smolensky market, train stations? It has to be a sense of duty one way or the other, but as duty has repelled me since I was born, without realising it (out of self-defence) I turn it all into an adventure

Subsequently she noted: 'What do I like about adventurism? The word.' An excursion to Tambov province in the hope of extracting food supplies from suspicious and tight-fisted country people on September 3rd and 4th formed the basis of the later essay 'Free Passage'.

*

A letter, dated from Moscow on February 27th 1921, in which she informs her husband about Irina's death has been preserved. Sergey made an undercover visit to Moscow to bid his wife farewell before leaving on January 18th 1918 to join voluntaries who were preparing to fight for the Whites at Novocherkassk. On May 12th he wrote to Max and his mother Pra in Koktebel': 'I have lost any connection to Marina and my sisters, I am convinced that they have long given me up for dead, and the idea leaves me no peace,' continuing: 'Our situation now is difficult – what to do? Where to go? Can it be that all the sacrifices were in vain? The idea is horrendous. I wait impatiently for your telegram and letter'. In a letter to Tsvetaeva dated October 26th

1918 (Old Style), he writes:

> I waited for you 5 months in Koktebel', writing not fewer than fifteen letters during that time, begging you to come here with Alya as soon as possible. Apparently the letters either didn't reach you, or circumstances were such that you couldn't leave... Trotsky has closed the frontier definitively and no one is allowed to leave Moscow under penalty of death... I hope that Nikodim, as always, will rescue you... My last and greatest request is that you stay alive.

Nikodim is the Polish economist Nikodim Akimovich Plutser-Sarna (1881–1945). In 1941 Tsvetaeva claimed that many of the later poems in *Milestones* were addressed to him, together with a considerable number written afterwards. Presumably his is the accent she refers to in the poem which heads the current selection, 'From your arrogant Poland'. In a letter preserved in her notebooks, dated October 1918, she firmly announces that she no longer loves him:

> For two years, mentally, within my soul, I dragged you behind me along every road, in every room, church, railway carriage, not for one second did I separate from you, I counted the hours, waiting for the bell to ring, lying there as if dead when it didn't – like everybody else in all of this – and nonetheless, not like everybody else.
>
> I can see your sunburnt face above the coffee cup – in coffee, in tobacco fumes – you resembled velvet – I mean your voice – and steel – I mean your words – I admired you, I loved you immensely.
>
> A comparison – bizarre, but absolutely accurate: for me you were the beating drum which aroused, at midnight, all the heroic youngsters of the city.
>
> You stopped loving me first. If that had not happened, I would still love you now, for I always love until the last possible moment.

> To begin with you came at 4, then at 5, then at 6, then at 8, then you stopped coming at all.

Tsvetaeva and her husband would not be reunited till she and Alya finally joined him in Prague in August 1922. For nearly four years she remained uncertain as to whether he was alive or dead. Ilya Ehrenburg delivered a letter from him in February 1922. In an extended prose piece about the work of the painter Natalia Goncharova (1891–1962), published in three parts in Prague in 1929, Tsvetaeva paradoxically affirmed that, where creative work is concerned, the most unfavourable circumstances may be the most favourable. Her productivity during the years of the revolutions, the civil war and "war communism" was certainly astonishing. They form the background to what was beyond doubt the single most prolific period in Tsvetaeva's career, during which she published not one book. She would write to Boris Pasternak on February 10th 1923:

> And – it's funny – seeing *how* they wrote (poems), I started to take them for geniuses, while I, if not a nonentity, was – an oddity of the pen, more or less a prankster. "How can I be a poet? All I do is live, enjoy things, I love my cat, I cry, I dress up – and I write poems. Take Mandelstam, for example, or Churilin – they're poets." Such an attitude took hold of me, I raised no objections, it did for me – and nobody paid me any attention, that's why from 1912 (I was 18) till 1922 I didn't have one single book, though in manuscript I had no fewer than five. That's why I am, and will remain, unknown.

Ten years later, writing to Yury Ivask (April 4th 1933), the perspective is substantially unchanged:

> In a nutshell: from 1912 to 1920, while writing uninterruptedly, I did not appear in print, because I had no time for literature, or rather, had nothing in me of the *man of letters* (that social manifestation of the poet) – *not*

even one book. Just an occasional poem in the St Petersburg *Northern Notebooks*. I lived, the books lay around. Not fewer than three *big, very* big verse collections failed to materialise, that is, they were never published.

Tsvetaeva was able to draw on this material when in 1922 she started publishing again. *Milestones 2* (Moscow 1921), actually preceded the first *Milestones* (Moscow 1922), and was the collection that brought her poetry to the attention of an astonished Boris Pasternak, while *The Craft* (Berlin 1923) features secretive, at times resolutely inward-looking, even solipsistic poems from a later stage, written in the years and months immediately preceding her emigration. If at certain points they read almost as if written in a private code, this could be due to the effective danger of holding, never mind expressing, political views and affiliations like those of Tsvetaeva in the Soviet reality of the time.

In 1923 Tsvetaeva did the very best she could to persuade two publishers in Berlin, Helikon, then Manfred, to take a book of extracts from her notebooks. The second word of the title is peculiarly difficult to render adequately in English. It could be "omens", "signs", "indices". I would propose the admittedly anachronistic translation *Earthly Credentials*, in the sense of characteristics which allow us to assign a phenomenon to a particular place and origin. The intervention of Roman Gul' was fruitless, however passionately she wrote about the book to him in a letter from the beginning of March 1923:

> Moscow 1917–1919. What do you imagine? That I was being rocked in a cradle? I was age 24 to 26, I had eyes, ears, hands, legs: with those eyes I saw, with those ears I heard, and with those hands I chopped wood (and wrote!), with those legs from morning till night I went around markets and checkpoints – wherever they took me! There is no *politics* in the book, but the passionate truth, the utterly passionate truth of cold, hunger, anger, of that *year*! My younger daughter died of hunger in a home – that too is "politics" (a home run

by the Bolsheviks)... Ah, Helikon & Co. Aesthetes! Not wanting to get their little hands dirty!... Not even for one moment is it a *political* book. It's a living soul caught in a deadly noose – and still living. The background is grim, but it wasn't me who thought that up...

She also put together two collections which failed to see the light of day during her lifetime, *Youthful Verses* (Paris 1976), with poems written from 1913 to 1915, and *Where Swans Are Camped* (Munich 1957), which offers us Tsvetaeva's own, very personal and specific viewpoint on the Russian civil war. A large number of items remained uncollected, many only achieving publication in the 1990s, when comprehensive editions of her work were brought out in New York and in Moscow, drawing in part on manuscript materials which did not become generally available till the archive put together by Tsvetaeva's daughter at last became accessible in 2000. In Véronique Lossky's estimation, there are 48 uncollected items for 1917, 87 for 1918, 86 for 1919, and 97 for 1920. The present book brings together poems written between August 1917 and October 1918, including 12 items from three cycles in *Psyche* (Berlin 1923) which did not find their way into any other collection.

*

On one of those dramatic train journeys to Crimea a fellow passenger recited to Tsvetaeva several poems by Pavel Antokolsky (1896-1978) of which she thought highly. Upon returning to Moscow, she lost no time in tracking down their author and, through him, was introduced to the troupe at the Third Studio of the Arts Theatre, working under the direction of Yevgeny Vakhtangov (1883–1922). He is the dedicatee of 'A seraph and an eagle! There's some fight!' and very likely also the addressee of 'You stand alone before so many beauties,/ confronting one hundred and thirty Carmens'.

In a manner not uncharacteristic of her, Tsvetaeva's attachments here did not concern one single person. According to

Simon Karlinsky, Antokolsky was at the time in a gay relationship with Yury Zavadsky (1894–1977), though later both men would marry and pursue distinguished careers in the world of Soviet theatre. They are presumably the two she imagines discovering in a sleeping embrace at the start of 'Brothers', part of a strand running all the way through Tsvetaeva's work which expresses her affinity and instinctive solidarity with gay men, accompanied here by delicious satire of her own enthusiastic subjugation. Tsvetaeva wrote (in *A Tale of Sonechka*):

> Pavlik had a friend he was always telling me about: Yury Z. 'Me and Yury'... 'When I read it to Yury'... 'Yury keeps asking me...' One fine evening he brought Yury to meet me. 'Marina, this is my friend Yury Z,' placing the same emphasis on each word, cramming each one full with meaning ... And that same evening, which became – the depths of night, which became – early morning, after parting underneath my poplar trees, I wrote verses to the two of them...

'One is a fop who's knocking at death's door' may also portray a gay pair, one a *roué* feigning studied indifference, while the other is a consumptive who does not have long to live.

At the studio she also met the actress Sonya Holliday (1894–1934) who, like Zavadsky, became the addressee of a cycle of lyrics not fully assembled till long after the poet had died. Having learned in 1937 of Sonya's death from a letter written by Alya, who had returned to the Soviet Union, Tsvetaeva spent the summer writing her most extended prose work, the *Tale of Sonechka*, a retrospective account of what has been termed her "theatrical romance" with members of the Third Studio. In 1918 and 1919, she wrote no fewer than six verse dramas prompted by her frequentation of them. And nonetheless, a brilliant consideration of the difference between a poet and an actor implies that she was never blind to the inherent doubleness, even falseness, of their cavortings and the roles which they assumed. The sequence devoted to Zavadsky has in Russian the title 'Komediant', not so far from the implications of the contemporary English word "playacting":

> Theatre people loathe the way I recite my poems. "You're ruining them!" They're the ones who fail to understand, itinerant peddlers of verses and feelings, that the poet's task is different from the actor's. What poets must do: having revealed, conceal. For them the voice is a cuirass, a mask. Without its covering they are naked. Poets always kick over the traces. Like water, the poet's voice extinguishes the fire (the line). A poet *cannot* declaim: it's shameful, offensive. Poets are hermits, for them the stage is a pillory. Offering one's own poems through one's own voice (the most perfect of communicators!), exploiting *Psyche* for *success*?! The substantial compromise of writing and publishing was already enough for me!
>
> I won't be the impresario of my own shame!
>
> Actors are different. The actor comes second. If the poet is *être*, then the actor is *paraître*. An actor is a vampire, ivy, an octopus. Say what you will, I will never believe that Ivan Ivanovich (and they are all Ivan Ivanoviches!) manages to feel like Hamlet every evening. The poet is Psyche's prisoner, the actor wants to take Psyche prisoner. In the last analysis, poets are ends in themselves, rest in themselves (in Psyche). Put one on a desert island – will they cease to exist? But what a miserable spectacle – an island, and an actor!
>
> Actors are for other people, inconceivable without them, people make them actors. The last applause, the last beat of the heart.
>
> Actors deal in time. They need to hurry. What matters is using – what's theirs, what's other people's – no matter. A line of Shakespeare, fleshy thighs – it all goes into the pot! And you want to make me, a poet, drunk on this suspect pig-swill? (I'm not talking about me, on my behalf, but on behalf of Psyche!)

No, my dear actors, we have different realms. For us – an island with no wild animals, for you – wild animals and no island. No wonder in olden times they buried you beyond the cemetery wall!

*

Lyrical sequences, verse dramas, extensive notebook annotations, verse collections, as well as long poems setting out from and transfiguring beyond recognition the folk motifs on which they are based – it would be a mammoth task for any individual mind, or reader, to get an overall view of Tsvetaeva's immense productivity in the course of these disastrous, yet triumphant years. The importance of the lyrics gathered here should not be underestimated. Each offers a modest, unassuming gateway to the immense world of her imagination and her travailed, eternally questioned and endangered humanity, even those with a missing word or phrase she did not find the time, or sufficient concentration, to locate and craft amidst the overwhelming flow of inspiration. Like the events which formed their background, these poems raise ethical and human issues to which no simple answers can be found. And when Tsvetaeva announces, as the winter of 1918–1919 approaches, that 'It befits heroes to be frozen', she prompts us to consider the nature of her own, idiosyncratic heroism, at a stage when the very worst was still to come.

Budapest,
March 2022

From your arrogant Poland
you brought me flattering words,
a cap of sable fur,
hands with tapering fingers,
bows, tenderness, the crown
on a prince's coat of arms.

But I brought you
two silver wings.

August 20th 1917

A woodcutter has felled
the murmuring young grove.
The plan which God laid down
has been settled by men.

The trees no longer sway –
just stumps, covered in mould.
Midst native tones I hear
your sombre, alien voice.

I keep seeing the wondrous
dark disks of your eyes.
They cannot part us two –
inseparably opposed.

August 20th 1917

Somebody left with a head on
a gleaming plate. Could it be me?
I'm hugging, as I'd hug a corpse,
an entire city, gone insane!

It has a fish's eyes, which gaze
at the horizon, glazing over;
above the city, evening bells
and sensuality, dull clod.

August 22nd 1917

Sleek-tongued fashion victims, we have not
come together to throw passion's party.
Cold and hunger are our sole tormentors –
humiliating, hideous Calvary.

Leading a life of sin, constantly drunk,
tearing Holy Scripture into tatters,
voluptuousness approaches – as if in
a gondola, on a Venice canal!

A rose consummate gardeners devised,
caught sight of through the fence around a church,
paradisiac wine that lovers drink,
voluptuousness, blossom of the blood!

Pour forth, inspiring fluid, in abundance,
Tokay wine, in answer to our longing,
a tribute to voluptuousness that never
fails, to blissful, heavenly luxury!

August 22nd 1917

No way! Hunger for love has not
yet parted these young lips of his.
He's tender – because of his youth,
he's tender – because empty still.

But wait! Upon those childish lips –
two rose petals out of Shiraz! –
a whole array of cannibals
will hone the edge of beastly fangs.

August 23rd 1917

JOSEPH

The courtier has gone off to court.
His slave bends over a dry crust.
The courtier's young wife has become
so bored she smashed her casket open.

She bit through doves' crops with her teeth,
pinched her maid from top to toe,
now takes hold of the young slave's swarthy
hands and pulls him close to her.

"Whatever makes your eyes so sad?
Our cellars hold an emperor's wines!"
The distraught youth: "I'm prone to visions,
and my master's faithful servant."

"Forget the man I'm married to!
The sun burns hot, he's far away."
"I serve a master whose immense
eyes don't flicker for an instant."

*

Long drawn out barking from the guard dogs,
a breeze wafts from the almond grove.
Voices that murmur in dispute
arriving from the sleeping alcove.

"I'm in charge of my master's purse."
"Women, coins – different matters, slave!"
"You're his diamond. How could I dare
cause offence to my master's jewel?"

*

Joseph's strife. Compared to this,
Jacob's hand to hand was nothing!
Smiling, the courtier's young wife
swallows so as not to wail.

August 22nd 1917

We looked each other in the eyes – no more.
We merely raised our voices towards a wail –
it was as if an iron glove had come
down on our throats, in the law's name, to force
tears back into our eyes, water onto
the banks and curses back behind our lips.
The freethinker is toppled from the bridge's
parapet by a freedom of wrought-iron.
An iron wing descends upon the ribcage
behind which lie our murmurings and groans.
Gripped within the towering law's tight circle –
there alone I find space, peace and light.

August 25th 1917

Blatant hunger's how I foot
the bill for my last grand outlay!
The last thing I could sell I placed
in a pawnbroker's withered hands!

God keeps a separate account
for estates squandered after dark.
Mine crashed. I simply lack the means
for extras such as nights or lips.

Let's say an unequivocal
and quick farewell – my hands not knowing
how to rob – senseless excess,
passion, excess of senselessness!

September 1st 1917

Without God, without bread, without a roof,
instinct with passion, ringing bells and glory,
the condemned prisoner with a darkened brow
leads his young wife to Siberia.

In days gone by, they went on deck at midnight
to gaze their fill on Chios and Izmir.
Marble tables in the coffeehouses
of capitals chilled their hands rich in rings.

What long discussions concerning the charms
of passion they had while a violin played!
The features of the foreigner vanished
in the faint smoke of Egyptian tobacco.

Along the highway to Siberia
beneath a sky low and indifferent
the gentleman who comes from foreign parts
leads his young wife onwards to their home.

September 3rd 1917

Bothered by a light so late?
No need to be concerned, kind sir!
I just can't get to sleep. No-one
good-looking and alone can sleep.

Insomnia's no burden for us,
since birth we haven't paused one moment.
We never get into a state.
It's better this way. We'll have time.

No yawns, no aches or pains. My son's
asleep, my friend is on his way.
He'll take good care of the mother,
God can look out for the son.

If it helps, for as long as I
can't cope alone, that's how I'll split
my woman's life, as God has willed –
the day my son's, the night my friend's.

September 4th 1917

I've not forgotten the first day, infantile ruthlessness,
gulp following on languid gulp, the whole divinely blurred,
our hands moving without a care, the heartlessness of hearts,
all of it thudding like a stone – a hawk – into my arms.

Look at me, quivering, transfixed with pity, feverish –
all I can do howl like a wolf, throw myself at his feet,
head hanging, grasp the penalty for sensual delight –
love innocent of pity, passion like a spell in jail.

September 4th 1917

PETER'S HORSE LETS FALL A HOOF

(fragment)

Trembling with passionate arrogance
some palm lifted into the sky
an incandescent crescent moon
which a horse of bronze let fall.

September 1917

One is a fop who's knocking at death's door,
the other close on twenty, destitute.
One talks, the other gasps for breath. One was
an angel, the other *will be* a devil.

They come to watch the trains arrive and leave,
listen to <...> in the deserted church,
while all the time his gaze is sunk in those
wide eyes, just like a lady's, or a woman's.

And still the younger of the two's unable
to catch the breath he needs, convulsive lungs
avidly gulp the smoke from a cigar
together with the city's midnight fogs.

The fallen angel briefly nods his head,
his store of blasphemies having run out
and, gazing at the streetlamp, the two say
goodbye, the older and the younger friend.

September 6th 1917

At evening families emerge
to take their places on the benches.
The tavern belches coffee fumes.
The gentleman gives her his word.

Pigeons are cooing. Now the pretzels
do the rounds triumphantly.
A small boy pulls a splinter out.
The gentleman kisses a rose.

Meerschaum pipes are puffing smoke,
neighbours thrust caps down more firmly,
talk of a skirt, and talk of teeth,
talk of a russet broody hen.

A scraggy youth with straggling hair
composes execrable verses
on the pain of separation.
The gentleman kisses her hand.

<…> are sleeping, children too.
Spinning wheels whirl, cradles rock.
The sailor spins a tale, the hunchbacked
tailor stands up, strokes his fiddle.

A pallid drunkard from afar
beats his cane upon his ribs,
proclaiming: "All of us are brothers!"
The gentleman kisses her skirt.

The bell tolls midnight from the tower:
'Good night!' all of them cry. 'Goodnight!

'May you enjoy good health!' 'You too!'
(The gentleman kisses her eyes).

Fun and preoccupation sleep.
The great hump on the fiddler's back
has fallen prone beneath the oak.
The gentleman kisses her lips.

September 6th 1917

So, hundredweights of cares having been loaded
onto the camel's hump – onto a good one –
the camel's meek and haughty – we depart,
bent on a task that's far beyond our powers.

Our camels' bodies heavily weighed down,
we dream about the Nile, delight in puddles,
as ordered by our master and our God –
carrying our cross with a camel's patience.

And when dawns start to glow above the desert
humps will be sore, and merchants start to puzzle
about which illness could so suddenly
afflict a docile and obliging beast.

But onwards the camel proceeds, no hint
of pleading in its eyes – its lips are parched –
until the Promised Land comes into view,
a greater hump lifting above the rest.

September 14th 1917

Eyemek Gwaroozim – the valley of roses.
A Jewish girl and a Spanish grandee.
Deciphering a fraying folio
engrossed you, only seven years of age.

Bowls of roses picked in paradise
transferred their conflagration to your eyes.
Moon over Saragossa. A black cloak.
A monk. A figure in a lengthy shawl.

Surrounded by her marriageable friends,
the Jewish girl's a rose amidst the gorse!
The silver cross that was her ancestors'
has given up its place to David's shield.

The beauty of your tresses, that dark gaze
have traced a shadow circle round your eyes.
Amidst the Bible's letters, a whole grove
of roses picked in heaven's blossoming.

Eyemek Gwaroozim – under that name love
revealed itself to you for the first time.
That was the name of the first book you read,
that's how tigers pick up the smell of blood.

Tensing your slender body for a leap –
how dark your eyes are! – you read on, learning
how, on the orders of a monk, they both
were burned at midnight at a single stake.

September 18th 1917

Oh, the fragrance
of your cigar!
Of your dark brown
cigar!
Rings, feathers, eyes,
panama hats…
dark-blue night
over Monaco.

An odd fragrance,
somehow fusty,
in the west a
bright red haze.
A streetlamp and
the thundering Thames
and then what more?
What more?

Vienna, yes!
Perfumes and hay,
a public scene –
betrayal!

September 23rd 1917

White, like the flour which they grind,
black, like the soot which they clean,
God will give a certificate
to millers and to chimney-sweeps.

But to half-hearted, disobedient
servants such as we are, black
millers and white chimney-sweeps –
Your Day of Judgement will be fearsome.

Black on white on that black day,
our place will be the pillory.

September 30th 1917

ROUEN

I walked in, then, and hailed him: "Greetings, King!
The time has come to turn homewards to France!
I'll set you back upon the throne again
and, seventh Charles, again you'll play the cheat!

Tight-fisted, cheerless, there's no point in waiting,
my bloodless prince, with stooping, feckless shoulders,
till Joan loses all interest in her voice,
till Joan loses all interest in her sword."

Next came Rouen, in Rouen the Old Market…
A re-run of the whole: one last glance from
my horse, then guiltless brushwood starts to crackle
and, catching fire, the pine logs start to spit.

Behind my back my winged associate
will whisper yet again: "Sister, endure!"
while my silver armour starts to glitter,
spattered with the pine blood from my bonfire.

December 4th 1917

Gardens fill with blooms, then fade. The wind
of meetings blew – now parting blows, a gale.
Of all rituals there's one I value most:
kissing the hands.

Cities stand unshaken, so do homes.
Young women are apportioned beauty so
they're driven crazy, so they can drive cities,
homes crazy too.

Music pours from all of the world's windows,
Moses' bush can't stop producing flowers.
Of all the laws there's one I value most:
kissing the lips.

December 12th 1917

There we stood, the two of us,
holding hands upon the bridge,
my own darling navy cadet,
not more than middling in height.

The mist was lying low, the sea
yawned like a chasm, evil, wild,
fury had possessed your captain,
your vessel sped upon its way.

I was on the journey home,
pouring myself lethal rum.
Cadet, cadet, my own cadet,
doing your service at sea!

December 22nd 1917

from THE GREATCOAT

5

Chevalier de Grieux, don't waste
time on dreams of your entrancing
Manon, a despot, a tyrant
with everybody but herself.

In a relaxed and languid column
we make our exit from your rooms.
The day after, and we're forgotten.
Raise no objections – it's the rule.

We come from stormy nights of snow,
the only thing we ask of you
being dinner – and perhaps some pearls
and, who's to say, your soul as well!

Honour, duty – rhetoric!
May mistresses queue up for you!
My dedication knows no limits
and I love you dearly – M.

December 31st 1917

6

Beau ténébreux! You're ill. Depressed. The world's
unfair to you. A sore tooth! Black as night,
a foulard hides your cheek's soft, yielding curve.

Faintly tinkling beads from Venice, given
by Casanova to a nun who broke
her vows for him, a steel blade from Damascus,

bells pealing for Epiphany throughout
a sleeping Moscow – nothing of all this
is able to dispel your present gloom.

Entrust the night that lies ahead to me.

A lantern is concealed beneath my shawl.
It's half an hour exactly since the clocks
struck midnight. You've no inkling who I am.

January 1918

7

Machinations of nocturnal swallows –
greatcoats – heroes fitted out with wings
seeking adventures in a world of snobs.
Greatcoat, looking smart even in tatters,
good for freethinkers and for unfrocked monks,
camouflage for a cherub or a rogue.

Greatcoat as capricious as a fleece,
so prone to going down on bended knee
doing its best to win our trust – night falls …
The watchman's horn sounds by the thundering Seine.
Casanova's greatcoat, and Lauzun's,
domino of Marie-Antoinette.

Look! Demon conjured up from forest depths,
the greatcoat's an enchanter, a whirlwind,
a crow hovering above the piebald flock
of butterflies from a world of *poseurs*.
Greatcoat colour of dreams, of times gone by,
adorning Cavalier Cagliostro's shoulders.

April 10th 1918

8

I bid farewell to Albion's foggy shores… —Batyushkov

"I bid farewell to Albion's foggy shores…"
Ah, divine altitudes! Ah, divine sadness!
I see featureless water's rippling bosom,
a sky that's featureless yet so familiar;

leaning against the mast that proclaims freedom,
wrapped in an overcoat, handsome as in
a dream, the youth. Shed tears, maidens, shed tears!
Manliness, misty Albion, shed tears!

It's done now! Alone with the sky, the sea!
A lesson for you, who detested schools!
The lord of fateful winds can thrust his way
between those fateful ribs, breached by a star.

Featureless water's rumbling is a ballad
of how he died, head branded with a star…
Weep, youth, love, world! And sob your heart out, Hellas!
Weep, little Ada, murky Albion!

October 30th 1918

I saw the new year in alone.
I, who am rich, was destitute.
I, gifted with wings, was cursed.
Somewhere many hands were linked,
Abundant vintage wine was drunk.
But I, gifted with wings, was cursed!
I, nobody else, was alone –
like the moon in the window's eye!

December 31st 1917 (old style)

BROTHERS

1

They lie asleep, still hugging close.
Brother – with brother.
Friend – with friend.
Together, on a single bed.

They drank together, sang together.

Wrapping them in a tartan plaid,
I gave my heart to them forever.
Through closed eyelids I discern
tidings that are strange in import:

a rainbow is a twofold glory,
daybreak is a twofold death.

I won't uncouple that embrace.
Before I do,
before I do,
may the flames of Hell consume me!

2

Two angels, brothers robed in white,
mounted on foaming white steeds!
Your silver armour blazes over
all the days left in my life.
And, because you both have wings,
thirstily I kiss the dust.

Soft, musical chiming of bells –
the tinker wanders with his tray
across the plain, the blind man with
his knapsack… Beneath your clattering
hooves, shards of Chinatown and of
the Kremlin smoulder, blaze and roar!

Two horsemen! Two paeans in white!
I met you in a maddened circus
ring. An archangel in curls,
blaring on a trumpet, and
one lifting over Moscow's realm
an arch whose substance is a rainbow.

3

I gulp my salty tears back down.
The novel, still uncut, was foolish.
There's no call here for slaves or roses
or for bright lipstick on my lips,

for lace, for white bread, for the sun's
light falling across angled roofs.
The archangels dashed off to Heaven,
the brothers caught the train to Paris!

January 11th 1918

Wind resounding, wretched wind,
fragrance of roses from the graveyard.
<…> child, cavalier and dandy.

A vicar with his holy book –
each <of them> lovely <in his way>
above the orphan's dissipation.

Only you, prodigal brother,
don't let the poison reach your mouth,

hiding the roses of your lips
behind mocking and carefree talk
and behind your coat's fur collar.

January 13th 1918

You're leaving for a distant land,
your heart will grow chill. – No it won't.
Bad travelling weather, nomads, dawn,
the woman at your side is young…

Who scattered roses on the snow?
It's nothing but mandarin rind…
Words keep returning in your head:
mazurka – death – marine – Marina.

February 1918

You stand alone before so many beauties,
confronting one hundred and thirty Carmens,
each carrying a flower between her teeth,
each of them asking to be given the part.

They all have feverish glances and red,
fawning lips, they all long ardently
for furs and fragrances, they are all virgins,
and every single one's a primadonna.

Their youthful eyes do penal servitude
in front of the footlights – the curtain falls,
the clapping's thunderous, scented silk enfolds her,
someone or other starts kissing her hands.

Grimaces, small change, inspiration, grease-paint –
and then the pub, cruelty, on show for sex –
the morning bells peal three o'clock, a head
is lifted and a voice heard pleading: 'Love me!'

February 19th 1918

A greatcoat for all who
are tall and well-built,
a greatcoat for all who
gaze into the East...

It must be five or six o'clock. A blue-grey haze. Day breaks.
The drinking bout lasted all night, until the seventh hour.
Demon-like, a greatcoat flaps up high over the bridge.
A woman or a demon? A Dominican's black robe?

A tenor from the opera? A widow's humble shawl?
Hiding a playful intrigue? Final journey to the pawnshop?
The urge to kiss. A siren wails. Gaga aristocrats
shuffle towards their beds, the dullard destitute towards Mass.

March 8th 1918

Epoch of crowned intrigues, epoch
of ruffians and greatcoats, for
crowned heads a Golgotha, epoch
when *philosophes* wrote manuals
for courtesans, and something moved
a fop from the *beau monde* to give
his life up for the greater good.
Beyond the ocean, Lafayette
flashed his sword of rhetoric.
Duchesses of highest rank
disarmed admirers, following
the heart's dictates, and Rousseau's too,
bathed in seas of childlike lace.

Little girls rolled hoops along
and nuns whispered to uniforms
in Tuileries awash with scent…
Meanwhile the queen, a humming-bird,
wrinkling her forehead, talked
to Cagliostro until day broke.

March 11th 1918

from POEMS TO MY DAUGHTER

4

"Thank you, Marina, for the world!"
My daughter says the strangest things!
And, high above her pale blonde head,
the heavens' vault has opened wide.

Lips twisted, harsh. "I won't admit
how much I love this, though it kills me!"
That's how the Lord of Sabbath hosts
hearkened to David from the sky.

Good Friday 1918 (April 20th Old Style)

5

(i)

I don't know where you end and I begin.
We sing the same songs, we have the same fears.
That's how deep our friendship goes,
the deprivation we two share.

It's great being just the two of us:
without a home, sleepless, bereft…
Two little birds who sing on waking up,
two wanderers whose nourishment's the world.

(ii)

From church to church we go, not caring whether
it's a small parish church or a cathedral.
From house to house we go, some of them poor,
while others are noble, with lordly ways.

Gazing one day, bright-eyed, on the Kremlin's
towers, you told me all at once to "Buy it!"
Since you were born, the Kremlin has been yours.
Sleep on, my luminous, fearsome firstborn.

(iii)

And as beneath the earth the grass
befriends the vein of iron ore,
two cavities, intensely bright,
detect a rift in heaven's abyss.

"Prophetess! Tell me why my child
was gifted with a similar fate?"
"Her fate is Russia's. And she got
the same years, the same rowan trees…"

August 24th 1918

7

As if you were a baby bell
you are delighted by the air.
Like you, its voice is delicate,
the bright dome's filled with little stars.

Your tiny cupola is golden,
beneath your forehead, two bright stars,
your little voice is delicate,
you yourself are a baby bell.

October 1918

Groaning passion, groaning death
and above all groaning – sleep.
A throne above all other thrones,
a law superior to all other laws.

Where there was wasteland, now a field
of rye, and rivers flowing blue...
All you need to do, young lad –
lower your eyelids!

Honey flowing through the veins.
Who goes there? It's him, it's sleep,
he knows how to wipe away
sweat of passion, sweat of death.

April 24th 1918

Sleep with his sickle passes by,
death passes carrying his scythe –
emperor and empress, brother and sister.

– Into the front hall, into heaven!
– Right into grandfather's barn!

Our way led along blue rivers,
our way led through wildernesses,
pilgrims going to the shrines.

– We have no room for you here!
– We have no room for you here!

– I'm an orphan sent by Christ!
I know how to open doors
with little keys for little locks
or with a handkerchief of silk!

– Our wanderings led us to you.
– On your way now! God be with you!

– My house is grandiose,
my honey famous,
my roses crimson,
my vineyard – flourishing…

Bread, anyone? Bread?
The yard's full of firewood!
Look up in the sky there –
little birds flying!

April 25th 1918

to Yevgeniy Bagrationovich Vakhtangov

A seraph and an eagle! There's some fight!
Accept the challenge? Up beyond the clouds!
In this year of blood and thunder, to
receive death at an equal's hands is glorious.

God's wrath has kicked us out into the world,
so that people will remember heaven.
The two of us can meet on Holy Thursday
at the church of Saints Boris and Gleb.

Moscow, Palm Sunday 1918

The pussy willow's glimmering down –
I, too, am soft and glimmering –
helps me to measure out the leagues
on God's highways, and his abodes.

Pussy willow, heaven-dweller!
Together skywards! Just you wait!
When you lay me in the earth,
put pussy willow in my hands.

Palm Sunday 1918

A star can vindicate a snake,
heaven the poor and bashful, water-
falls can marshes, bread a stone.
The Marseillaise the mob, cala-
mity the tsar, their grave mound those
who stood firm, and a rose their mound...

May 9th 1918

"Forgive me, my mountains!
Forgive me, my rivers!
Forgive me, my cornfields!
Forgive me, my meadows!"

His mother placed a cross around his neck
and bid farewell forever to the soldier…
One more time, inside the crumbling hut:
"Forgive me, my rivers!"

May 14th 1918

A rich man fell for a poor girl,
a man with schooling for a fool,
a red-cheeked man for a pale girl,
someone good-hearted for a scoundrel,
a sovereign for a penny farthing.

Where, merchant, are your fineries?
"In a basket full of holes!"

And you, so stuck up, where's your learning?
"Underneath my girlfriend's pillow!"

Fine-looking man, your scarlet cheeks?
"They melted away overnight."

The silver cross with the small chain?
"My girlfriend put her boot on that!"

Rich men shouldn't love poor girls,
or men with schooling love a fool,
red-cheeked men shouldn't love pale girls,
men who're good-looking fall for scoundrels,
golden sovereigns for penny farthings!

between May 21st and May 26th 1918

The Lord endowed me with
a cheerful, stalwart heart,
the gift of tears and song.

He shielded me
with a white banner,
but denied me
flesh's bright flame.

The banner soars
on high – where He is!
Heavier than stone
flesh's bright flame.

May 1918

You'd like to know what makes me rich?
Racehorses are meant to race,
the dead to sleep, and birds to chirrup,

the young to rummage frantically
and senseless womenfolk to weep.
The gift of tears – that makes me rich!

May 1918

I rinse the linen in the brook,
plant and water two little flowers.

The bell chimes – and I cross myself,
they set me fasting – I obey.

My hair's as silken as my soul.
My good name's worth more than my life.

I live according to God's laws
but, wolf and thief, it's you I love!

between May 26th and June 4th 1918

Young men are ablaze,
young men blush bright red,
young men shave their beards.

Old men have regrets,
they must warm their beards.

(I woke up with these lines on June 4th 1918)

A cautious knock, three times repeated.
Dear enemy, despairing friend,
I'm not deceived! No wanderer's path
ends here. That knock is seeking love.
That's how black Hell, with lowered eyes,
knocks at the gate of brilliant Heaven.

June 6th 1918

I am. You'll be. Between us lies a chasm.
I drink. You thirst. No way can we agree.
The two of us are ten years, are a hundred
thousand years apart. God builds no bridges.

My command is: "Be! Let me pass by,
not troubling your growth even with a breath."
I am. You'll be. Ten springs from now you'll say:
"I'm here". And my answer: "But that was then…"

June 6th 1918

Breadcrusts, suffering – the price is high!
All we munch, the hole inside a pretzel.
Walking the highroads with a bulky basket
frightens you – then what about your soul?
Coins out of sight and wares amidst the rushes…
But there's no way you can conceal your soul!

June 6th 1918

When I lie dying, I won't say "I was",
or entertain regrets, or look for culprits.
In the world are matters weightier
than passion's tempests or prowess in love.

Beating against these lungs with your young wing,
you, instigator of my inspiration,
the one thing I ask you to do is "Be!"
My obedience will never falter.

June 30th 1918

Nights without the man I love – and nights
with one I don't love, and above a fevered
head gigantic stars, and hands stretched out
to one whom centuries could not create,
who can't and won't exist, although he should.
The child cries for the hero, and the hero
cries for the child, and great mountains of stone
weigh down on him whose fate it is to sink...

I know whatever has been, or will be,
I know the whole deaf and dumb mystery
which, in the dark and slurring language used
by human beings, carries the name – Life.

between June 30th and July 6th 1918

I spoke, a second person heard and whispered
to a third, who understood, a fourth
took out an oaken walking stick, set off
into the night to do heroic deeds.
The world has made a song of this, and I
– oh life! – face death with that song on my lips.

July 6th 1918

REMEMBERING BÉRANGER

A catastrophic mother! Day by day
my reputation merely gets more dreadful.
A rascal takes me revelling,
writing makes me neglect my firstborn child.

Envying the empresses of fashion
and little mites of dancers wearing tights,
I contemplate years passing at the cradle
and fail to see that the milk's boiling over!

Which of you hypocrites refused to stuff
himself, or paid the bill, at times like this?
I take my patron's bottle as my witness –
your patron too, at some stage – Béranger!

Despite upheavals, rowdiness, despite
frivolity, one thing – I remained faithful.
My dreadful reputation, get it right –
catastrophic mother, faithful wife!

July 6th 1918

Air redolent of incense. Passing rain.
From the houses' gaping maws, a grand
piano's thunderous, scurrying roulades
tear the July night apart.

The city is revenged thanks to the thunder
of Beethoven's heroic storms…

<between July 6th and 10th 1918>

I am the page your pen writes on.
I'm white, I welcome everything.
Store for your wealth, I give it back
multiplied one hundred times.

I am a village, fertile soil.
You are the sunbeam, drenching rain.
You are the Lord and Master, I
both gleaming clod and snow-white page!

July 10th 1918

Remembering you is like thin smoke,
wisps of blue smoke outside my window.
Remembering you's a peace-filled home
where you live, under lock and key.

Wisps of smoke, did I say? A home?
The floor takes off beneath my feet!
The door's unhinged! Beyond the ceiling,
through blue smoke to the peace-filled home!

July 10th 1918

My day is wanton and absurd:
I beg for bread from a poor man,
offer alms to a rich man,

thread a needle with a ray,
hand the house keys to a thief,
use talc to redden pallid cheeks.

The poor man doesn't give me bread,
the rich man won't accept my coins,
the ray won't go into the eye,

the thief enters without a key,
a fool, I shed buckets of tears:
day without glory, without sense.

July 27th 1918

Midday lies leaden on the village.
Thunder of departing hosts.
Haughty, tender, not a woman's,
a blissful voice hails from the clouds:

"Onwards to torment by fire!"
Clothed in rippling sheep's fleece,
I raise my hands towards the sky
as, long ago, a certain girl…

July 1918

The heavy forehead droops, droops further, like
an ear of wheat that's waiting for the reaper.
Indifference has nothing to teach you, friend!
All it does is render hearts unfeeling.

The reaper is good-hearted, reaps and binds,
the field is soon covered in grass again…
But God chastises those who are indifferent!
One mustn't trample on a living soul.

Love that finds no outlet suffocates.
Love's spare change will be enough for me!
Indifferent friend, how awful to hear black
midnight chiming in an empty house!

July 1918

Some ears of corn are loaded, others scraggy:
God's flail makes no distinction, strikes them all.
On the cathedral square I saw a beggar,
close to a hundred, asking for some bread.

A century-old beard! He has forgotten
some things young people lack are worse than bread.
You beg for old age, grandad, I for youth!
God's flail makes no distinction, strikes us all.

August 5th 1918

Young folk need spare no thought
for stooping age.
Old folk need not recall
youth's blessedness.

Waves carry it all off.
That sea's not yours.
Forgetfulness, pour over
human heads!

Wrinkled passer-by,
no point admiring sails!
And young folk, there's no point
in admiring old age!

Some turn to sand, some go
to school. To each his own…
Forgetfulness, pour over
human heads!

Young folk with golden fleece,
don't learn from age!
That's a murky affair,
murky, senseless.

…Forgetfulness, pour over
human heads!

August 9th 1918

Night's a nun, a female felon.
Night goes past with downcast eyes.
She breathes in panting, heavy breaths.
She doesn't like you watching her.

She holds no candle in the temple,
she's no-one's wife, and no-one's daughter.
She sleeps the night through on hard stone,
doesn't give anyone a kiss.

No point in whistling
when we're in tears,
no point in each of us
roaming the world –

no hope of escape!
Sooner or later
night, the aged
procuress will
catch us napping!

August 9th 1918

Day is a broadly rustling cloak,
night a fur coat soft as velvet.
Some have their wits about them, others
don't. It's up to you to choose!

Friends! Give a fanfare from your trumpets!
Friends! Decide which trees will be felled!
Sleep has tucked a fur coat, soft
as velvet, close around my lips.

August 12th 1918

You don't like me, nor do you,
you neither, nor does a whole horde,
Abundant hair – her clothing's scanty!
Ringing tones – but so ill-natured!
Don't debase yourself, Tsar-Maiden!
Dogkeepers are mean – not tsars!

August 14th 1918

Verses proliferate, like stars and roses,
or beauty which the family has no use for.
Only one way of answering the gift
of garlands, godhead – "Where is this all from?"

We're sleeping, and the heavenly guest arrives
through slabs of stone, within a four-leaved clover.
Grasp this, world! In a dream, the poet learns
the law of stars, the structure of a blossom.

August 14th 1918

My refuge from the savage hordes,
my last resort, my shield and cuirass
against ill-will from good and bad –
you, verses lodged in my ribcage!

August 16th 1918

Next they gave me mead to drink,
after that came penny ale
so that, kneeling by the gallows,
I'd admit that I'd committed
crimes in which I had no part!

They rendered wine loathsome for me,
They rendered food loathsome for me,
come now, champion, and defend me
from such abundance – you, spade!

August 18th 1918

TO HER DAÏMON

They christened us in the same font,
placed the same garland on our heads,
harassed us with the same confinement,
branded us with the same brand.

We will be lodged in the same house,
one mound will cover both our heads.

August 18th 1918

You are alien yet familiar,
no relative, and yet related,
mine and not mine! When I call
upon you, I am not "a guest",
and yet I can't say I'm "at home".

Love is like a fiery furnace,
and yet a ring's a thing of weight,
an altar is a blinding light –
nonetheless, God withheld His blessing!

August 26th 1918

The forehead lifted towards the sky
is haughty and beyond reproach.
Coats of arms mean naught to me,
the grave offers no cause for fear.

Caught between slaves and potentates,
hunchbacks and insignia,
where foreheads dig into the earth,
the oak tree is my next of kin.

August 26th 1918

Where honey lies, a sting lurks, too.
where death awaits, there's also daring.
I can't say what provoked the meeting
and yet it happens, song ensues.

An oak tree stood tall in the meadow
then suddenly crashed to the ground!
With no accompaniment of female
moaning, of a woman's howl

I say goodbye to you,
say goodbye to myself,
I say goodbye to fate.

August 26th 1918

Who failed to build a house
does not deserve the earth.

Who failed to build a house
will find no place on earth,
neither ashes nor straw...

I failed to build a house.

August 26th 1918

Writing and breathing
get simpler and simpler,
sharper and sharper
seeing and hearing.

Less and less scope for
remembering, loving.
They can't be far off now –
walking-stick, tatters.

August 26th 1918

No need to talk to me. Here are
my lips: give them to drink.
Here is my hair: stroke it. And here
my hands: feel free to kiss them. – But
best thing of all, just let me sleep.

August 28th 1918. Feast of the Assumption

An officer strolls by with his sabre,
a student strolls by with his book.
For every young man we're a servant –
women, made to be their slaves.

With their boots they trampled on
the small flowers planted in the garden.
We will not speak of what we saw –
women, indifferent as fish.

September 9th 1918

EYES

Eyes inured to the steppes,
eyes inured to shed tears,
green and salty
eyes of a peasant!

If I'd been a woman of the people
I'd have paid to have a place to sleep
with those green
eyes, filled with fun.

If I'd been a woman of the people,
my hand would have shielded me from the sun,
rocking back and forth in silence,
my eyes fixed upon the ground.

A lad passed with his tinker's tray…
Sleeping beneath a monk's headscarf,
those staid and serene
peasant's eyes.

Eyes inured to the steppes,
eyes inured to shed tears,
peasant's eyes don't betray
whatever they witnessed!

September 9th 1918

You arrive – at the table's edge
a slice half eaten – one I left,
a glass half full – one I was drinking,
<…> – I looked at.

Sit down here on the scarlet bench,
eat and drink – don't judge too harshly!
I've done both and now I sing,
feeding an eagle from the steppes.

September 28th 1918

Place two flowers here upon
my heart, where they can breathe for me
so I'll look good when I set off –
my repose is well-deserved.

In the year <...>
I had two daughters in my care.
Getting flour was constant torture,
you had to queue for everything.

Death approaches, takes a look –
most diligent of gardeners –
says: 'God will offer his reward.
This fig tree wasn't without fruit!'

September 30th 1918

These gifts were given me from the heavenly heights:
a sword of silver and a soldier's cross.

I was vouchsafed a chant for Eastertide:
"Joan! Maiden, Empress! Rise up and begone!"

Destined to overcome worlds, there rose up
consecrated flesh in a knight's form.

Arms open wide, I expose my bared breast,
acknowledging what's at the heart of things.
I undertake to burn up high, then fall.

October 8th 1918

Remove the pearl, my tears are left.
Remove the gold, the maple's autumn
leaves are left. Remove the purple –
I still have my blood.

October 9th 1918

Love! Love! Where have you ended up?
I abandoned my wealthy home
and donned a soldier's coat of mail.

I'm nothing now but Voice and Rage.
I became the Maid of Orleans.

October 10th 1918

Autumn. An avenue of trees, like soldiers,
Each has its own particular smell.
                              God's army.

October 14th 1918

You're the full moon, Persian girl, the crescent moon's a Turk.
You fell into captivity while he, he rides a horse.
Your cheeks are flushed with red, full moon, while he is sinewy,
yellow-skinned from birth, like Knowledge and Nobility.

I'll remain faithful to you, Friend, as long as they both shine:
the full moon out of Persia, and the Turkish crescent moon.

October 14th 1918

Morning. Time for washing cups,
for watering the roses.

Midday. I hold an olive's swarthy
flesh between my fingertips.

A bell rings. So it's four o'clock.
A voice. An angel bringing news.

Roses watered a second time.
More bells. The flush as day declines.

Night, and a cast iron grille
descends. Voices at war with wings.

October 15th 1918

Dearer to me than anything
was the balmy garden air
in a monastery where
nuns and widows would resort:

nuns once mothers in their time,
who entered exile willingly.
I realise the blessedness
of quiet and of melancholy,

the blessedness of handicrafts
and the charm of firm foundations –
dearer than anything to me
was the balmy garden air.

In a year that can't be known,
severe, unbending, there will lie
in the convent garden a
dame many knights paid homage to!

Dearer than a monarch's treasures,
dearer than Casanova's eyes,
dearer than everything to her
was the balmy garden air!

October 15th 1918

Daughters make their hoops spin round,
mothers do the same – with hearts.
Along the road a column lifts,
composed of dust from hearts and hoops.

October 15th 1918

I'm not a troublemaker, I won't pour
you woman's poison out to drink.
I offer you a faithful hand,
the one I write with, my right hand.

The one I use at night to bless
what I hold extremely dear,
the one I use when writing down
the words which God dictates to me.

The other hand's impertinent,
flattering, audacious, sly,
not like the one I offer you –
steadfast, deserving of trust!

October 23rd 1918

It befits heroes to be frozen.
Cold is stately, just like me.
Hail to you – white desert world!
Heroism of the winter!

A white rider's my closest friend,
my life now – forehead to the snow.
At last I can sing winter's praises
in the year nineteen eighteen.

October 23rd 1918

Notes

Joseph The tale of Joseph and the wife of Potiphar, a captain in Pharaoh's guard, also included in the *Quran*, can be found in *Genesis* 39: 5-20, while the struggle between Joseph's father Jacob and the angel is recounted in *Genesis* 32: 24-29.

Peter's Horse Lets Fall a Hoof The bronze statue of Peter the Great in the Senate Square in St Petersburg was inaugurated in 1782 and is the subject of a celebrated poem by Pushkin dated 1833.

'At evening families emerge' Meerschaum pipes were produced from sepiolite, imported from Turkey, with Vienna being a major centre of production. Their introduction in place of clay pipes dates from 1723. Tsvetaeva wrote of this poem in 1939: 'For me, a German village in the 18th century. The poverty-stricken, drunken foreigner is a Frenchman – *liberté, fraternité* and suchlike.'

'So, hundredweights of cares having been loaded' Tsvetaeva's notebooks contain the following entry: 'Members of the bourgeoisie were forbidden to use horsepower for clearing snow. So, after brief consideration, they rented a camel. And the camel saw to it. The soldiers laughed in appreciation: "Good for you! That's how to get around the decree!" (I saw this with my own eyes on the Arbat).'

Rouen Joan of Arc, barely 20 years old, was burned at the stake on May 30th 1431. Another evocation of this figure, not dissimilar in spirit to Tsvetaeva's, can be found in Jules Bastien-Lepage's splendid canvas of her visions in the Metropolitan Museum of Art, New York.

The Greatcoat As published in *Psyche*, the cycle also features three poems from *Milestones*, 'Yet again', 'A female adventurer, a man' and 'A thin flap from a hooded cape', the fourth poem in the cycle 'Don Juan' ('Don Juan always had a sword'), the opening poem in the cycle 'Playacting', dedicated to Zavadsky ('An evening comes to mind. Early November'), and two poems from the end of 1920

('Please don't let anybody know my name' and 'Hair like short wings is what I can remember'). The Chevalier de Grieux and Manon Lescaut are the protagonists of the famed French novel first published in 1731. The Duc de Lauzun, Armand-Louis de Gontaut, later Duc de Biron (1746–1793), took part in the American War of Independence and also commanded the French Revolutionary Army, before being executed at the guillotine. His memoirs were first published in 1822. (6) is addressed to Zavadsky. The quotation from Batyushkov (1787-1855) heading (8) is from a poem to a friend who perished in combat. Ada was Lord Byron's daughter.

Tsvetaeva put together in 1939 another cycle entitled 'The Greatcoat' from 'It must be five or six o'clock. A blue-grey haze. Day breaks' and 'Epoch of crowned intrigues, epoch', between which she inserted 'Machinations of nocturnal swallows'. The Marquis de Lafayette (1757–1834) played a prominent role in the American War of Independence, the French Revolution of 1789 and the revolution of July 1830.

As published in *Psyche*, the cycle *Poems to My Daughter* begins with 'From cloud to cloud', 'Four years old' and 'Along paths gently resonant with frost', and continues with 'We take the road of ordinary folk', then 'From her blouse run through with silver threads', 'I never lift a finger when you fall', 'Sooner or later, creature of enchantment' and 'Consuelo! Consolation!'. The third and eighth poems also feature in *Where Swans Are Camped*, Tsvetaeva's collection celebrating the heroism of the anti-revolutionary White forces. *Psyche* further featured 20 poems written by Alya herself.

'A seraph and an eagle. There's some fight!' A note in the manuscript indicates this poem is unfinished.

Remembering Béranger Pierre Jean de Béranger (1780–1857) was a celebrated French poet and songwriter whose wildly popular songs, critical of the restored Bourbon monarchy, twice led to periods of imprisonment.

'I am the page your pen writes on' Tsvetaeva noted in 1939: 'One of the best poems in the book' and, quoting it in a 1931 essay, observed: 'Did I realise then, in 1918, that in comparing myself to what is humblest (fertile black earth and blank paper) I was naming what is greatest – the bowels of the earth and all the possibilities of a blank page? That, with all the ingenuousness of somebody in love I was simply comparing myself to – everything? Did I realise it – and did he? 1918–1931. One correction. You should only talk like this to God. For this is a prayer! You don't pray to people. 13 years ago I didn't know this yet – no, I knew it! – but stubbornly refused to know. Once and for all, all my poems of this sort, such poems in general are addressed to God.'

'You don't like me, nor do you' The idiom Tsvetaeva quotes in the final line generally implies that, in a society organised hierarchically, the people immediately above you count more than those who are at the top. Yet it is possible that here she provocatively reinstates the literal meaning. *Tsar-Maiden* is the title of one of the long poems based on folklore motifs she wrote during these years.

To Her Daïmon Tsvetaeva uses the Russian cognate of the Latin "genius", presumably in the sense of a guiding or inspiring spirit rather than of a highly gifted individual. The Greek term "daïmon", indicating a benevolent guiding spirit, is preferred here to avoid confusion.

In preparing these notes, reference was made to the Russica and Ellis Lak editions of the poems, as well as to the first volume of Véronique Lossky's bilingual edition, Poèmes de Russie *(1912–1920). Information given in the introduction is not duplicated.*

www.ingramcontent.com/pod-product-compliance
Lightning Source LLC
Chambersburg PA
CBHW031401160426
43196CB00007B/844